lost in the 4rest:
experiments in kishōtenketsu

lost in the 4rest:
experiments in kishōtenketsu

garrett ray harriman

2016

Copyright © 2016 by Garrett Ray Harriman

All rights reserved. This book or any portion thereof may not be reproduced or used in any manner whatsoever without the express written permission of the publisher except for the use of brief quotations in a book review or scholarly journal.

First Printing: 2016

ISBN 978-1-365-29762-5

www.short4orm.wordpress.com

for everyone I love

contents

introduction: surprise, surprise - 1
a note on 4orm - 7

I

silence - 11
awe - 13
view - 15
monkey - 17
home - 19
tenacity - 21
weight - 23
release - 25
legacy - 27
steal - 29
routine - 31
lesson - 33
love - 35

II

warmth - 39
beast - 41
rest - 43
snafu - 45
glasses - 47
legend - 49
endurance - 51
flicker - 53
road - 55
rarity - 57
child - 59
ideal - 61
talent - 63

III

future - 67
song - 69
heron - 71
magic - 73
grief - 75
light - 77
itch - 79
mistake - 81
fame - 83
voice - 85
vice - 87
gratitude - 89
kindness - 91

IV

tree - 95
past - 97
ennui - 99
train - 101
date - 103
memory - 105
chase - 107
struggle - 109
loss - 111
secret - 113
wind - 115
bloom - 117
patience - 119

acknowledgments - 121
about the author - 123
farewell - 125

introduction:
surprise, surprise

We've all been "there." My "there" was summer, 2015.

It had been a year since college graduation. My mental, physical, and financial lives were in various states of collapse. My handful of friendships had evaporated like spoiled milk. My spiritual self, plucky recruit though he was, had gone AWOL. I probably smelled.

You know...*there*.

At this point in time, for whatever reason — likely the result of some late night Internet-diving nostalgia-fest — I remembered a name: Hayao Miyazaki. A few quick searches reminded me he was the beloved Japanese animation director, the touted "Walt Disney of the East." An hour later I found myself transported by his film *Kiki's Delivery Service*, a gem of a movie that follows the daily coming-of-age tales of a witch in training.

This was my launch pad into the art and culture of Japan. I was greedy for knowledge. I started learning Japanese, reading Japanese authors, investing my brief, *per diem* hours of stable mental energy researching the customs, the culture, the art of Japan. I chased after this foreign high with passionate abandon. My darkest summer soon became a whirlwind of audio-visual delights. In a strong, redefining way, I felt I had trekked an escape from a country of crushing dangers into a homeland I'd forgotten, but always knew I'd find again.

I was floored by the surprise of it. Japan had saved my life.

In the midst of this experience, I felt an urge to return to writing. Even brief, once-or-twice-weekly blog posts, I figured, might provide me with some growing plot of solid ground: ground on which I could plant my newly woven Japanese banner.

But what would I write about? I dug around a bit, rented some haiku books from the library, but nothing spiced my noodles. Then, on one freeform online expedition or another (Surprise!), I followed the veins of Eastern storytelling methods to a body, a form, which explained why a large proportion of Japanese art fascinated and resonated with me: *kishōtenketsu*.

Kishōtenketsu (起承転結) is an ancient Chinese poetical form. Verse written in this framework presents an idea (*ki*), develops that idea (*shō*), holds that idea in contrast against some new, surprising element (*ten*), and then resolves itself by hinting at a newly gained perspective (*ketsu*). Today it most popularly manifests in *yonkoma*, a type of 4-panel Japanese manga, though the concept at large is still integral to Eastern modes of thought, speech, writing, and film.

It's the inclusion of *ten* — the unexpected, the puzzling, the abrupt — which separates *kishōtenketsu* from Western written forms that sanctify conflict as the lifeblood of plot. Struggles of the "X vs. Y" variety are relatable to everyone, and Western storytelling has bottled and distilled their essence for centuries. But life, by-the-by, is more capricious and less Hero's Journey the majority of the time.

For instance, most people's hours unfold in very *kishōtenketsu*-esque fashion: episodes of normalcy, periodically invaded by moments of uncommonness, which are then either reconciled or ignored. The form is a steadfast reminder that stories, both personal and fictitious, can operate without engines of violence at their centers, relying instead on the everyday fuels of juxtaposition and unpredictability.

This is also why the form is so powerful: it defamiliarizes the arbitrary march of existence. *Kishōtenketsu* reflects our cumulative daily experiences, infusing them with the humble wonders and glaring inconsistencies hustled past in our perforated 9-to-5 patterns. It champions those mundane, modest, and misleading aspects of human existence, our quotidian chores and habitual natures, and makes them seem *vital* again. Because, of course, they are.

This was it. It had to be. I revved up WordPress, resolving not to abort this endeavor like the half-dozen other blogs I'd created and abandoned over the years. I'd experiment with this writing tradition four sentences at a time, some cross between flash fiction, prose poetry, and haiku. My posts might be vignettes, or transcend genres, or evolve into some interconnected chain of scenes caging together a single story. I had no idea. I had no polestar. All I had was the desire to begin.

Thankfully, as my Sunless Summer came to a close (itself, unfortunately, morphing into Sunless Fall and Winter), short4orm.wordpress.com remained a fragile, gleaming Japanese oasis for me, and remains so. It also attracted a modest, curious, and supportive following who encouraged me to keep going. And now, a year later, it's encouraged me again to stitch together this book.

Life is a struggle, without question. Those "theres," those uncharted, unfeeling valleys, are perennial and necessary pit stops for all of us. But life is also a mystery machine, a feather that tickles, a joke that throws us off balance. Daily grinds and disarming surprises are more than just the interstitial fabric connecting once personal conflict to another. They are the bulk and beauty of life itself.

Kishōtenketsu invited me to rekindle my amazement at the universality of the unexceptional, and thus replant my feet during a harrowing time in my life. What's more, writing these pieces over the past year has made me respect just how many kinds of surprise exist and are essential to the human experience. There's the surprise of contrast, of sudden appearance or disappearance, of character and counterpoint and metaphor and turn-of-phrase. There's the surprise of fumbling head-first into a country and culture you never knew was part of you.

And there's the surprise of dogged perseverance wrought by the delightful antics of a stubborn teenage witch. Who knew?

I hope this book surprises you.

Thanks for reading.

Garrett Ray Harriman,

July 2016

a note on 4orm

Each of the 52 pieces in LOST IN THE 4REST is four sentences long and embodies *kishōtenketsu'*s internal parts (introduction, description, twist, conclusion). They present self-contained worlds, moments, or emotions held together by shock, wonder, or counterpoint. Presented together, their goal is to offer a brief, vivid glimpse into the possibilities of non-Western narrative.

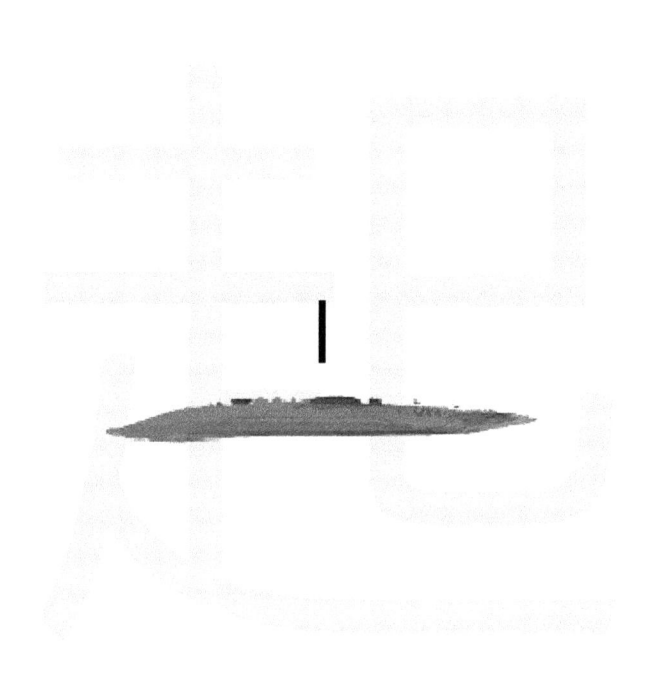

silence

Her grocery cart squeaked a path to the bank of self check-out machines. Boxes and cans poured from right hand to left, each barcode emitting a mild, forsaken boop. Unclipping her billfold, the realization dropped like a turbulent plane — no other consoles booped, no other carts squeaked. She craned her head in silent alarm toward the lot beyond the glass, listening.

awe

They carried the bottle rocket to the top of the hill, the child and the man. Their hearts leaped and howled at the marvel of the thought: their homemade fuselage harpooning the moon and stars, bursting the mellow summer night to life. Fire ate the fuse to the brink of launch when the man charged the grass, tackled the toy, and exploded in a carnival of jewels, each the size of the child's front tooth. The treasure was heavier than the child anticipated, warmer; it was hard skipping home with every pocket full.

view

I've been busy. So busy. Yesterday a bird ricocheted off my office window, broke its neck (presumably), then fell twenty stories and stained the pavement with feathers and blood (again, presumably — I didn't leave my desk). Tom, my office mate, just reminded me this room has no window.

monkey

I hadn't visited the zoo in decades, but my child's heart still drew me to them first. The liveliest enclosure housed the capuchins, and I watched their troupe leap and swing and roughhouse for several hours. During a lull when no school tours swarmed the glass, one of the patriarchs stood, captured me in its stare, pantomimed slicing its throat, then fell back into play with its underlings. Next day I joined an elder fitness group, just to prove the hairy devil wrong.

home

A ghost once lived in a beautiful house. It swept the floor and set the table, removed the trash and rocked the crib. Eventually the little girl outgrew her dollhouse, but its ghost, dutiful and kind, sustained the eviction with pious resolve. Its presence has become a family heirloom, a subtle force pushing in the chairs of each new girl's imagination.

tenacity

Rain clouds spiraled above the empty garden. The woodpeckered remains of a scarecrow's stake wavered limply in the breeze, tossing its withered shadow over parched crowns of soil. He'd caught the lizard outside the post office two evenings past, and already its tail, severed in an effort to give the slip, had begun to regrow. A tough fist of wind plucked the stake from the garden's center, the shallow hole it left behind soon plugged by muddy water.

weight

The movers stepped out of their van, affixed their belts and back braces, and rang the customer's doorbell. With relief in her eyes, the lady of the house led them through the foyer, past the kitchen table, up the stairs, and into her daughter's old bedroom. A young woman sat hunched beside the open window extracting heavy, invisible objects from her head, tossing each find into the nearest cardboard box, towers of which tickled the ceiling. With professional aplomb, the movers tipped their hats, rolled up their sleeves, and tag-teamed the first of the baggage: a shoe box-sized number no lighter than a star.

release

A man takes a walk before lunchtime. Passing through the vacant park, he watches a stranger on a bench silently collapse onto the ceramic autumn ground. He rushes over, fingers ghosting the emergency number in his phone, but the fallen stranger, more than okay, laughs like a worm-riddled jackal. Anger fills him, relief drains him — then the walker folds over, too, hysteric with joy, the distant clouds scattering behind the dying, gilded boughs.

legacy

Mice had bred to uncountable numbers, compelling the town's farmers to raid their hardware store for every last model of mousetrap. Barns and pantries for miles lay loaded to crack the scourge's collective spine, and the men and their wives slept soundly. None more soundly than the store owner's son; slighted too long for chasing dreams of apprenticing magicians, he'd swapped the deathtraps with gag shop models before eloping with the train ticket stitched inside his coveralls. Grain silos rang empty that season; the store owner boarded up shop, scurrying from the dark days his son had left behind.

steal

Car for sale. Minor dings and scratches, new snow tires for season. Left side mirror shows past, right side future, 5 years either way. Accepting immediate cash offer — discrete location preferred.

routine

Another endless drive-thru line. No radio, no date. A meteor the size of Istanbul skims Earth's orbit, recalculates its interest, then deflects to a more appetizing corner of void. "Dammit, I said no pickles," growls our hero, chucking his burger out the side.

lesson

"When I was little, my neighbor down the hall kept a window garden. Pretty standard botanical fare — tulips and marigolds and the like — but I didn't know that, and so diligently learned all their needs, their peccadilloes, and kept them company when she'd leave for family trips. Once, during a morning watering, my fingers unearthed a cache of sterling silver rings, then quickly folded them back into the soil. Catching me on stairwells, she'd often ask why I stopped coming by to check on her blooms, never realizing her hand in reshaping what beauty meant to me."

love

One walk home from school, she rescued a rabbit from an overflooded culvert. After its wounds healed and strength returned, the little creature no longer tolerated her advances of comfort, and spent its waking hours cowering in the far corners of its cage. "You can't force fear away, lovely," her grandma advised, "nor love to grow, but don't think for a minute they can't wear the same face." She remembers the night she let the rabbit go free: it hopped to the end of the lawn, ears draped and quivering along its back, its progress slow, minute, retreating ever farther from her heart.

warmth

Snow fell heavy on the old man's walkway. He geared up in the same coat and boots his father had worn all his life, resolving in his heart to shovel the path clear if it killed him. Long since those gathered had expounded on his gentleness and legacy, a surviving grandchild, in a fitting symbolic gesture, snapped and burned the cursed shovel. The coat and boots were kept; their weight and warmth eased many winters.

beast

The wind-bitten flyer read "Lost Dog" and profiled a large, mixed breed he'd never seen before. He considered some possibilities — *St. Dane? Huskeranian?* — then ripped off a callback ribbon to feel better about himself. His phone erupted as he turned the corner; the incoming string of digits matched the one now floating inside his pocket. Haltingly, he swiped to receive, but no voice answered — just the wet, tortured panting of a hope-forgotten animal, racing full-bore through the inner-city dark.

rest

And then the man and Sleep were not on speaking terms. Ten weary nights elapsed before the duo made their peace, though Sleep played the coquette, never admitting what went wrong. Around the block, a mother and father fell into bed, praying for an eleventh night of newborn baby slumber. Their angel wailed and wailed.

snafu

"Happy birthday to you! Happy birthday to you! 'Happy birthday's' a misnomer, actually — speaking ontologically, your creation involved no reproductive processes, and the genetic committee helming the parent project unanimously signed an NDA attesting to the utter fallaciousness of your existence, so, uh. . .jeez, sorry there, buddy. Cake's in the fridge, help yourself."

glasses

The man enters an eyeglass shop, approaches the woman at the counter, and asks to see the most expensive pair in stock. She obliges, reaching inside the shelf beneath her, and presents, with petite hands, a light and exquisite frame. The man slips it on, watches as her hands become hooks, then removes it, returning the model to her care. He utters thanks and exits the shop, feeling like he's forgotten his own pair inside — but of course, he wore no pair to begin with.

legend

The bird burst from its egg to be raised in the plumage of its mother's breast. It grew rapidly, as wide as the sun, until its mother could no longer shield it from the brightness of ambition. Without a home, the bird left Earth to find a suitable nest among the stars, but the planets and the moons silently refused its company. It drifts in darkness still, eager for a perch, unaware of the many worlds birthed and gathered by its passing.

endurance

"Oh, I'm fine, I'm fine." The universes of frustration, pain, and unrequited dreams shaping those words were infinite, but she said them anyway, each syllable a stubborn closet door refusing to let loose the Ironing Board of Truth. Along the parched African soil, regiments of dung beetles rolled their Sisyphean shit balls, aimlessly, all-consumingly, the succoring shade of marula trees brief and incomplete. "Anyway," she pressed on, "what's happening with you?"

flicker

She tumbled onto the groundskept football field, her body a glowing, surf-washed shell. She lived for these flashes of post-running bliss, when the grass, like a tide of victory, lapped its many waves against her skin. Above her, the cerulean sky endured, then, without violence, dimmed as she watched, no bird or cloud the culprit. The dimming continued day after day, biting at her heels like a chum-drawn shark.

road

"Remember no thing for its own sake, but for the ghost of a future self incomprehensible in this moment. Speak no thing for its own sake, but for the ears and wisdom of a child long forgotten . . ." The rain-starved hills welcomed his car's presence, its steely purr and pinpoint turns, as a kind of quenching liquid, some rambling flow of life on the run. The radio show ended, the DJ's prophetic words another snowdrift of white noise piling in space; the driver pulled over, kicked open, threw keys, walked off.

rarity

Imagine a short promontory jutting over an icy cape below, its surf like a thousand china shops shattering. A couple speaks loudly over the tumult, stopping as one on some psychically predetermined point whereupon they plant two folding chairs beneath a crystalline pelt of stars. She sees the first ones — snowflakes like dust motes against the night — before the summer flurry loses all inhibition. It lasts less than a minute, a freak, beautiful spattering hijacking their quintessential August night, and still, years later, when their own winters take hold, they remember.

child

"Never mind — just, never mind. Jesus, we're not having this conversation!" A wet mass of legs and auburn fur slides onto the forest floor; the mother deer takes a breath. "If you ever bring this up again, I swear to God I'll leave you."

ideal

The café stayed open, always. That was the rule — a rule forged *in medias res* World War II, kept alive by the taciturn, nostalgic exports of many an ex-pat author. The hunter skins the hide off a young doe; the process takes cold, cold hours, a supple hand, and tools with edges sharp as survival itself. He'll write out of this life someday, inventing conversations and trysts for characters to have in coffeehouses far away, reciting aloud, "It's the beans, not the bloodshed, dear girl, that won the fight."

talent

Her pupil's fingers traversed the piano like they were discovering new lands, making unearthly leaps over entire valleys of sound no ordinary child should have mustered. "Wonderful, dear," she praised, cupping his shoulders, "you're on perfection's edge." She let his music carry her to the world outside the studio, to the masses, virulent with deafening parasites, patrolling soundless streets. He played on, numb to the beauty abounding from his performance, while his teacher, all ears, wept against the window.

III

future

"Welcome to LifeSwap™ Station 7-B Alpha, a subsidiary of Existence Enterprises, LLC and the ReincarCorp® Genetic Catalog! LifeSwap™ prides itself on developing robust suites of proprietary FleshPaks© and MindMelds© guaranteed to last up to 85 years or half your genetic code back! Our records indicate your contractual limit for LifeSwaps™ (4) has been reached: Your current incarnation will expire in nine days, sixteen hours, and thirty-seven minutes! If you feel your TimeOnEarth® has been unduly curtailed, or that you are the victim of LifeFraud™, please direct all appeals to our friendly legal department (Average Response Time: 5 – 7 months)!"

song

I'd heard that the pipe organ was once the most mechanically advanced human invention in the world. What must that be like, I wondered, crafting something to shift the cultural sands, a precedent decreeing "Yesterday, void; today, the beginning?" After my usual walk around church, the arpeggios of a robin muted history's echoes from my head. *Birds need no precedent,* I thought — a simple thought — then whistled for the first time in ages.

heron

Silent, statuesque, the heron bides its time along the early morning floodplain. Each lifting leg thrums silver ripples through the cattails, alerting only the most sensitive fish to its calculating presence. The young surgeon fights panic above his patient; the robotic arm assisting him, an edifice of inhuman composure, assured and benevolent and uncomfortably, even vitally, alive, angles in closer. The heron lunges and misses, lunges and misses, its eyes dead-firm, its beak slitting the water's skin, the writhing fish consumed.

magic

"Let's throw our shinnies into the fountain, lovies, it's never failed me before. Look at it — long as a man, porcelain skin, four curled, clawed feet digging deep into the earth. Beautiful...though just think how more beautiful if the water could run. No, no, dear ones, that's my fool's heart talking — you wish for whatever you want."

grief

The old woman buys a bouquet of carnations and walks up the sloping cemetery hill. Every week for nineteen years, she's placed her bright offerings on a virgin plot of grass beside a line of foundering tombstones, a preemptive gesture of love for those yet untaken. Some days, visitors move the flowers to a neighboring grave, cursing the callous wind; others interpret a waste, tenderly plucking blooms to gift their other living halves. By week's end the flowers disappear, and the old woman, moved by mystery, returns.

light

"The candle, nurse, quickly!" Footsteps like wing beats brisk the hall, then the Queen, on her knees, feels a length of wax press her palm. Rather than light it, she bites and swallows two-inch lengths at a time, chasing the piecemeal torch with a still-burning match. "Will it see the beacon?" asks the nurse, splaying a quivering hand across Her Majesty's stomach — a stomach which kicks in reply.

itch

"God dammit!" she hisses, plucking the golden-up-until-thirty-seconds-ago piece of bread from the toaster. Around the corner, her father hacks and wheezes in the living room armchair, his aged morning chorus a time bomb for the rest of her day. She ignores the knife's shaking in her hand and slathers strawberry jam from blackened edge to edge while, as ever, the old man's foot itches, has not stopped itching for five years, smothers his mind in nothing but bone-deep, insufferable itch. They eat at the coffee table, their crunch-chew-crunch a screaming rift between them.

mistake

You know when you reach for a pencil, botch up, then realize you've accidentally written in pen? Then you rummage for more paper but discover, of course, the last sheet's the one you've butchered with ink, and there's still no pencil, and now you have an ultimatum to face? I'm now confident time travel adheres to the same set of principles. So if you've found this apology, Future Earth, kindly take note of the eraser marks.

fame

A hush smothers the apartment after the parrot finally speaks. Two whole floors have gathered to bear witness to its final thoughts, words to be forever enshrined upon the building's spinsters' throw pillows and the lips of its latchkey kids. See the gypsy girl laugh at the man's muted pleas to return his voice, her promise of their transmutation, their power, to be lost on the wings of an unseen bird, brief and meaningless as the wind. The cockatoo's coda — "Life is a lie you tell yourself!" — survives its Internet upload, infects the world's many screens, then nothing.

voice

"Come closer, my darling; there's but little time between us, and my voice is a fading star. Lean across these covers, take my hand, feel my breath upon your ear, like before. Do you remember the hour you gave me this voice — your voice, darling? — how for years I hardly used it for fear of poisoning your generosity? Your muteness at my expense. . .it breaks the whole of me, darling, maddens me, even now, not knowing what your heart may have shouted inside my throat!"

vice

The apartment was small and mediocre and hers. She wondered in secret if she would live there until she died. Every night, her downstairs neighbor sprinted through her dreams, warning her against the vice of complacency. She got married, a promotion, a bigger TV, but the gentleman downstairs kept running.

gratitude

He squats at the end of a rain spout, a little boy aged 9 or 10, holding steady a blue plastic bucket. It's early; the storm awoke him before the rest of the house, and he's decided to do what Daddy used to do, only Daddy's bucket was metal and held more, and then Daddy took it with him, far away, but all the same he tries his best as the sky cries itself anew. "Son of a bitch," growls Mr. Three-Piece Suit, savagely mopping the milk off his tie before accosting the front desk staff for more napkins. He is all smiles — three times he fills his bucket, three! — until the cloudburst melts into tomorrow.

kindness

She said he'd know if she ever became rich because she'd spend all day patrolling city streets feeding change into blinking parking meters. "Some of my brightest days started after someone 'changed' my life," she proclaimed with a wink. The doctor applauded her kindness, held fast her arm, and escorted her back to her room. Months after her passing, no meters starve along the hospital.

IV

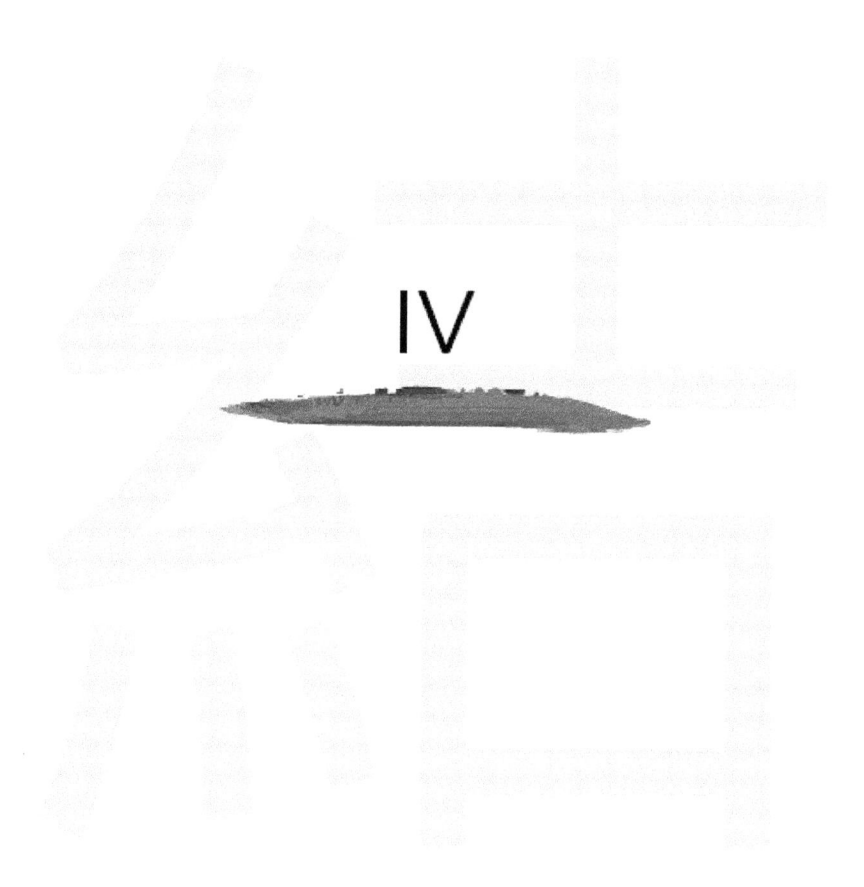

tree

The tree on the hill was always dying. From spring to spring it endured autumn's curse; old leaves puckered and fell, new leaves unfolded on naked limbs, gilded and ocher-veined. The house it eventually embodied was ever in disrepair, and a procession of frustrated owners impotently combated its sagging frame and crooked windows. From the ashes of the abandoned hovel now grows a blazing forest, a site of holy pilgrimage for lovers of Mischief and Death.

past

The fisherman casts his net into the morning-glow waters. He's used the same net since he was a boy, trolling the reedy banks with his father and brothers and selling their catches at market. The boat suddenly lurches — a young, familiar man flips himself aboard and untangles his limbs from the rope. "Let me take a turn" the visitor offers, but already the fisherman swims.

ennui

They were there, all right — the same pair of squirrels he'd subscribed to since September. He leaned back against the park bench, gnashed his dripping sandwich, and settled in to watch Chip 'n' Dale's Drama Hour unfold. Fifteen minutes in a crow dragooned the burlier rodent away, acorns a-flying, while the runt got bagged on its blitz across the meadow. "Stupid reruns," the man half-burped, wolfing a handful of Twinkies down his throat.

train

Winter months saw the train pass through town in a bedlam of whistles and spilled inkwells of smoke. Children, starved not least for entertainment, took to making bets and holding breaths, their daring game over whenever the weakest lunged among them broke the sooty clouds with a cough. "Over here!" shouted the lad who found them first: boot tracks zigzagging away from the depot, preserved in the locomotive's black snow, not a stride indented through the powder. That long season the juggernaut feasted, its every race beside the shanties claiming another mother's son.

date

She walks through the park with a homemade lunch. It's a boisterous afternoon — the lawns swarm with picnickers and "Tag, you're it!" kids. She pauses beside a man-shaped stamp of grass which rises and locks arms beside her. They reach the public fountain; she unpacks her meal, he picks her his flowers.

memory

The little boy fell into the lion pit. It took fourteen personnel two-and-a-half hours to bait and sedate the pride before they could extract the unconscious child and airlift him to the hospital. His mother calls on the anniversary of the fall, asking how things are, if he's eating well, and he recites in even tones how he rarely notices the scars, how he remembers nothing, which is the truth. He hears her own scars pulsate her voice, their breath inside her breath, before his daughter grabs the phone, telling Grandma about her super field trip to the zoo.

chase

Once, a man impersonated a piano tuner for thirty years. He had faith some baby grand, somewhere, would open a secret bookcase to him, denude its secrets, if he but played the requisite melody. The detective dedicated to his arrest dusted for fingerprints on thousands of ivory keys in hundreds of credulous homes, always a full step behind. Unlike his quarry, the music of their escapade never deafened the gumshoe's heart.

struggle

Sunlight stains the boat deck. The fishermen towel themselves dry, circling the corpse of a swordfish, patting themselves on their backs, cursing in jubilation. The general sees his imminent defeat writ across the valley, the June-bright hills saturated in blood and bodies and torment. "Let's pose for a picture!" prompts the captain; his vessel rocks a little harder.

loss

"Lunch, honey!" she called from the kitchen. With a practiced flip, she plated a grilled cheese sandwich, filled a bowl of steaming tomato soup, and balanced her way to his bedroom door. She knocked and entered, tiptoeing past hundreds of identical dishes, oblivious to the rotting, hot-box stench, and puzzled today's meal onto a corner of the empty bed. She closed the door behind her, mumbling, "That stubborn boy," then returned to the dining table and the meal she wouldn't eat.

secret

As a child, she loved exploring sea caves. Within them she learned the wind's many voices, the maternal softness of perspiring hollows, and how life can flourish inside pools no deeper than dents. In the house poised on the cliffs above lived another girl born deformed and dumb and blind. Unmet, they kept their seclusions to themselves; the ocean they shared bored its mass against the headlands.

wind

The town priest closes his bible, then signals assent to the hangman. The rope delivers its promise firmly: a clean drop, no writhing or drooling or death throes for the crowd assembled. In a faraway field of honeysuckle, a young girl and her mother collect flowers in a basket, severing each head from its hale, green stem. It's a beautiful day for it, the picking, though somehow the wind feels lost.

bloom

The man dreamed of boulders crushing him alive. For weeks he awoke under the weight of imaginary mountains; some mornings he shook dirt and earthworms from his hair. Red-eyed, thumbing through magazines at the doctor's office, he discovered a flower that only thrived in the churned earth of landslides, its roots most inspired beneath cozy beds of destruction. He ordered its seeds, popped them like Ambien, and fell into bed a hopeful gardener.

patience

Rain roared off his roof in perpetual, silvery sheets. Its mania frothed the narrow gravel road, beheaded roadside flowers, drowned thought. From the comfort of his chair he watched a hummingbird, trapped for the duration, wheel, lunge, and zoom the length of his veranda, its dire heart rejecting the storm's endless demeanor. "There's patience in the rain," he might have spoken, then gently returned to his book.

acknowledgments

Cover image: "Jomoku ni suzu" ("Bell hanging from a tree"), artist unknown, Library of Congress

Title image: "Ashibune ni tori" ("Bird and boat among reeds"), author unknown, Library of Congress

Farewell image: "A bird flying to the left, seen from above," Hokusai Katsushika, Library of Congress

Section heading image: "Collection of black paint stains" designed by Freepik

Back cover poem: Waka 87, Jakuren Hoshi, from *Ogura Hyakunin Isshu* (小倉百人一首)

eBook cover services: Canva & BeFunky

Font: Montserrat Light courtesy of FontSquirrel

eBook software: Scrivener

And a very special thanks to all of my WordPress readers, subscribers, and commenters!

about the author

Garrett Ray Harriman lives and writes in Colorado. He graduated from Fort Lewis College with B.A.s in English and Psychology. He plays saxophone whenever possible and enjoys learning languages. Several of his stories have appeared online, most recently at Dali's Lovechild and 365 Tomorrows.

To read more of his work, please visit him at

short4orm.wordpress.com

farewell